A PASTOR'S GUIDE TO EVANGELIZATION

Going to the Well
to Build Community

★★★★

Deacon Timothy E. Tilghman

GINGER —

THIS CODIFIES OUR LAST
CONVERSATION. WE
SPEND TIME MEETING
+ ASKING FOLK TO ACT
ON WHAT THEY BELIEVE.
THE JOY IS IN THE
ACT OF MEETING.
KEEP DOING IT. HOPE
THIS HELPS.

— Timothy.

acta

GOING TO THE WELL TO BUILD COMMUNITY
A Pastor's Guide to Evangelization
by Deacon Timothy E. Tilghman

Edited by Gregory F. Augustine Pierce
Cover and text design and typesetting by Patricia A. Lynch

Scripture quotations are from the *New Revised Standard Version Bible*, copyright © 1989 by the Division of Christian Education of the National Council of the Churches of Christ in the USA. Used by permission.

Published by ACTA Publications, 4848 N. Clark Street, Chicago, IL 60640, (800) 397-2282, www.actapublications.com

ISBN: 978-0-87946-580-3
Printed in the United States of America by Total Printing Systems
Year 25 24 23 22 21 20 19 18
Printing 10 9 8 7 6 5 4

♻ Text printed on 30% post-consumer recycled paper.

CONTENTS

* * * * *

Dedicated to Cyprian O. Tilghman

The defining role in my life is as a son, the son of an organizer. Going to the Well to Build Community *is about my striving to live the lessons of my father, as Jesus worked to do the will of his Father.*

INTRODUCTION

**Most folk take the free drink when it's offered.
Why not go to the well and get the best?**

*The Church will have to initiate everyone — priests,
religious, and laity — into this "art of accompaniment,"
which teaches us to remove our sandals before the
sacred ground of the other (cf. Exodus 3:5).*

Holy Father Francis,
Evangelii Gaudium (EG) #169

A pastor in Washington, D.C., once asked me about
hiring an organizer to help him with evangelization,
wanting to apply the organizing discipline of engaging leaders and mutual accountability to the task of
the New Evangelization. When he made the request,
I did not know that it would lead to a group of pastors meeting two hours every month over a five year
period to talk about how they could work together to
accomplish the mission of the Church. Clergy invited
lay people into the communal gatherings. Diocesan
staff described these mission-oriented communal
gatherings as a new paradigm. Clergy decided to
name their effort "MISSION IN MOTION." In this
little book, I want to reflect on how a focused conver-

sation about mission can be sustained.

For me, the conversation began around kitchen tables and in church basements in Washington, D.C., in the 1950s. I met the best people in the neighborhood in these places. Looking back, it was a joy to meet, listen, and learn. This was the Black Catholic Church in the neighborhood. This is what Mike Gecan; author of the *IAF Organizer Training Manual*, meant when he said, "All relating is meeting (not meetings)." Pope Francis recently captured the essence of relating and meeting with his phrase "the art of accompaniment," the one thing that every Christian is called to do for us to be Church, the Body of Christ, living and transforming the world.

※ ※ ※ ※

The conversation is a journey back through the old neighborhood. I remember walking to church, to school, or to a neighbor's house to deliver a few eggs, a stick of butter, something so that could be used to prepare a meal for the day. I remember walking past a classroom at Henry Smothers Elementary School and hearing a teacher say, "Mrs. Tilghman's house is always spick and span," and I wondered what the topic of discussion was in the classroom that day.

Besides the help with the day's meal, there were lots of good deals in the neighborhood. We could buy "two-for-a-penny" candy by collecting and redeeming soda bottles, or we could pick wild blackberries and take them to a friend's house to have them turned into hot and fresh blackberry muffins. The most valuable "two-for-one" bargain was discipline and instruction in neighborhood values. I could walk an hour in any direction from my house in the neighborhood and people knew who I was and would share conversations with me about my parents and twelve older siblings. If any of these folk discovered that I turned the wrong way when I was supposed to "turn right" according to neighborhood values, I got spanked on the spot! Without fail, someone was waiting at the door when I arrived home to deliver the other half of the "two for one." There was always a second spanking that preceded the lesson on family discipline and neighborhood values.

Miracles happened every day in the neighborhood. School teachers, postal workers, and folk who did domestic work and other manual labor lived in the neighborhood. Government was of, by, and for people. Housing assistance was often a "rent party." Food assistance was walking a few eggs, some butter, or plates of food to a family at the end of the block who were more in need than we were. Clothing assistance was "hand-me-downs." My parents sacrificed to send a few of us to the local Catholic school, and they fully engaged in life at local public schools to make sure that all their kids got educated. My mother knew every teacher who stepped into the classroom with each one of her thirteen children. And the greatest miracle of all in the neighborhood was that folk who had no car, no internet, no cell phone, and no house phone found a creative way to convey the circumstances of a breach of the neighborhood value system to our "aunts" and "uncles" who, though not related by blood, loved us as if they had brought us into the world personally.

This was my life in the neighborhood and my life in the local church; there was no discernable difference back in the day. I knew that our church was a church of the Civil Rights movement. How did I know? When Archbishop O'Boyle said that the Catholic Church of Washington would be fully integrated in the late 1940s, my mother took to heart the Church's teaching on justice and the dignity of human life, sending my oldest brother, Robert, to St. Paul's Academy in 1948, well before *Brown vs. Board of Education*. Robert wore his "hand-me-downs" to school each day, always neat when he arrived in the classroom after cleaning spit from his clothes from Whites who did not approve of his presence in the previously "all-White" school. Graduating from St. Paul's at the top of his class, he went to Catholic University of America, which was also not fully ready to receive Negro students in 1952, despite the Archbishop's mandate in the 1940s. Looking back, Robert's experience was my first taste of "relating as meeting" or what Pope Francis calls "the art of accompaniment," which I will try to explain throughout this book.

Robert's experience was shared, in detail, with all who attended Our Lady of Perpetual Help School or who were, in some way, connected to the neighborhood church, which was primarily staffed by Josephite Priests and Brothers. When the word about a breach in the neighborhood value system came to our house, it was Robert who received the word and dispensed the necessary discipline to his twelve younger siblings, to other youth at our parish, and eventually to all the students he encountered in Baltimore City Public Schools, where he worked for decades.

The lessons taught and modeled by my brother, along with countless aunts and uncles in the neighborhood, brought me to service in the Coast Guard, to community organizing, and to diaconal ministry. In the 1950s I did what I did because my parents told me to and and to avoid a disapproving look from Robert when I got home. Today, I do what I do because I realize that "relating is meeting," which is also the "art of accompaniment" of which our Holy Father Francis speaks.

But this book is not about me; it is about the Church, about being called to ministry and being sent (like an apostle) into the neighborhood. After twenty-three years in the Coast Guard and a brief stint as a management consultant, I went to see my father and tell him that I was going to work as a community organizer with Washington Interfaith Network (WIN), the local community organizing affiliate of the Industrial Areas Foundation, the premier network of congregational organizing in the world. Having listened to all of my musings about life after the military and about maybe going into politics, his immediate response was, "Tim, you just don't know *what* you want to do!" After I convinced Dad that I was serious, which was no small feat, he and I shared the best talk of our life together.

Talk about affirmation! I was surprised by my father's enthusiasm and every word from his mouth that followed. "Did you know that I was an organizer?" was his first question. After graduating #1 in St. Cyprian School's Class of 1929, he took the only job he could get, bellboy/elevator operator in the Harrington Hotel. When his peers decided to organize to build a union, my father was elected shop steward, accepting his first job as a union organizer. There were no unions in Washington, D.C., hotels when he became the shop steward, but most city hotels were unionized by the time he was elected a union officer in the late 1950s. Unions continued to thrive until his retirement in 1979. Now, he felt, the last of his thirteen offspring was, in a way, going into the family business.

Then, five years into my organizing work, I told Dad that I had been accepted as a candidate for the permanent diaconate at a youthful fifty-two years old! When I was accepted as a candidate, he bought me a gift that he had personally shopped for and found, a missionary cross. The gift said everything my father had taught me about important work. Through the conversation over many years, Dad taught me a most important lesson; there is great value in doing the Father's work.

My father found great joy in each one of my organizing struggles and victories, delighting in his youngest son's work both as an organizer and deacon of the church. He saw much of organizing my success: $70,000,000 invested in the poorest neighborhoods in the city, the construction of housing, the rebuilding of neighborhood schools and community centers, and the development of lay leaders who did the work in Catholic parishes and beyond. We talked about work in my parish often, as my father would go to his neighborhood sources to find out what I was doing in the parish beyond my WIN community organizing. He died in February 2009, one year before my ordination and departure from WIN, without knowing how my present conversations with pastors would expand and deepen.

I left WIN in January 2010 to start a two-year journey with the Josephite Priests and Brothers, experiencing the Church in the neighborhood in new ways that formed me on a larger scale by identifying and walking with leaders in the Josephites' forty parishes and twelve schools in Alabama, California, Louisiana, Mississippi, Texas, Virginia, and Washington, D.C.. While working for the Josephites, I also shared my burning question with pastors I met through community organizing and work in ecclesial movements in the Catholic Church. The question was and still is: If we could get $70,000,000 of investment in the poorest neighborhoods in D.C. by inviting leaders to act on their faith in their public lives in the neighborhood, what could happen if we used the same principles to build the Church in the neighborhood? The revelation in the experience is that people convinced of your willingness to meet them where they are will not only share but will act on their faith with you.

* * * * *

Going to the Well to Build Community is a reflection on the deep conversation that leads to relationships that bring people into the Church. At some time in our life, we have all been the Samaritan woman that Jesus met at the well in the fourth chapter of John's gospel. We were on the outside, looking to be invited into the conversation, feeling bad about our sins and shortcomings, and thirsty for the prescription to transform our lives. The Samaritan woman took a drink of the living water at the well, meeting the living Christ and changing her life in the process. Jesus met her where she was, and he quenched the thirst that she thought was unquenchable. The woman walked away from the well with a renewed spirit and the determination to share her encounter with Christ, the living water that had transformed her life. Those who heard her witness came to meet Christ and also witnessed to how a drink of the living water could transform their own lives.

So, if we want to receive what the Samaritan woman received, we have to go to the same well and drink the same water. We can't get the drink, which is free, unless we are willing to enter into and stay in the conversation.

* * * * *

This is not a theoretical conversation. It has to lead to action, and it has. Through a series of meetings over the past several years with clergy in historically African-American parishes in Washington focused on the need to build the Church, I have discovered that community organizing is similar, if not identical, to the "old time religion" that is at the heart of the ecclesial movements in our Church. ("I," the first person singular pronoun, is not the best to use when talking about this discovery, because all of the fruit produced came from the public witness of the communal gathering of clergy.) Clergy then invited others to join the conversation. Organizers would say that "relating is meeting." Ecclesial movements would use the label "small group meeting with mutual accountability."

Clergy in these historically African-American parishes described their situations as unique. Africans, Latinos, and young urban professionals are among those served. Gentrification, suburban sprawl, and demographic shifts are changing the face of the surrounding neighborhoods. People in the pews are more concerned with finding community than they are in staying within parish boundaries. Often, the people in the pews are not the ones who live in the surrounding neighborhood. This new situation is the state of the Church in and beyond the traditional African-American parish community. The two lessons learned in the conversation are these: the Church is always in transition, and Saint Augustine of Hippo was right—souls in the neighborhood are restless and will be restless until they encounter the truth, which is the risen and living Christ, who is embodied in the Church. The restless want to experience Pope Francis' "art of accompaniment," which is the invitation to join the conversation.

When faced with transition, folk are hungry for the truth embodied in the Church, the personal and communal encounter with the Christ who lives. Participating clergy link the action of sharing this living Christ to the New Evangelization. Our Pope Francis talks about the action throughout his treatise on evangelization, *Evangelii Gaudium (The Joy of the Gospel)*. Here are just three of the fruits of the conversation thus far:

- ***Communal Gathering of Lay Leaders.***
  Modeling a mantra from the Cursillo Movement, *"Talk with God about people before talking to people about God,"* clergy invested almost one year in conversation to determine the best way to invite lay people into the conversation. In February 2013, nearly 100 lay people from eleven different parishes responded to the invitation to join the conversation about a unified effort to accomplish the Church's mission. The laity departed with a renewed commitment to witness to one another and animated about improving the vital signs of life in and beyond their parishes. Energized by the encounters, participating leaders continue to work on the mission of sharing the encounter more than one year after being invited into the

conversation.

- **East of the River Revival after the Invitation to Join the Conversation.** After twenty-three "business as usual" annual revivals, clergy invited the Revival Committee leaders into conversation about a unified effort to focus the 24th Annual Revival on a greater commitment to mission-oriented actions. The results— improved attendance and full confessionals each of the Revival's four nights, and vastly improved clergy presence and participation. More lay leaders and more mission-oriented action initiated by the Revival Committee's lay leaders were incorporated into planning for the 25th Anniversary East of the River Revival. More parishes are participating in the event that originally included parishes from a single deanery.

- **Celebrating Marriage in the Neighborhood.** Responding to the call to action of the 2013 East of the River Revival, a team of married couples from multiple parishes outlined and implemented a strategy to strengthen marriages and mentor the newly wed and engaged with regularly scheduled "Marriage Reunions." On a blistering cold February 15, 2014, as the metro area was digging out from a blizzard, eighty people (married, engaged, and singles) from five parishes witnessed to each other about the joy of overcoming struggles to live the sacramental life as husband and wife and committed to continue the "Marriage Reunion" conversations. Subsequently, presenter-couples from Worldwide Marriage Encounter and the Engaged Encounter communities were excited to join and continue the conversation in their circles.

- *The Consequence of Doing What God Is Blessing.* Hearing the conversation about the "Marriage Reunion," the youngest couple at the table saw the need to invite their young adult single peers to join the conversation. This couple convened a cadre of young adult singles to engage and invite the young adult community into the Church. Engaging in the conversation is contagious. Youth and their ministers, ministers of charity, and men who look to invite other men—especially young ones—into the Church began to use the conversation. Archdiocesan ministers with responsibility for youth, young adults, marriage and family, and ministry to the African-American community joined the conversation with the idea to unify and collaborate instead of just offering the "headquarters' solution."

Working with the "Marriage Reunion" team and clergy, one of our pastors introduced the idea of *"doing what God is blessing rather than asking God to bless your work."* Taking this idea to heart, clergy and laity have come together to focus on the mission of sharing the encounter through practicing the "art of accompaniment." Why? I could say that it is community organizing; but that answer would be inadequate and incomplete. Like the Samaritan woman (John 4:4-42), people get animated about their faith when invited into a real conversation. People are moved by the clergy communal gathering. Each time clergy have invited leaders into a conversation, those invited have responded with great enthusiasm and creativity in practicing the "art of accompaniment."

For me, the most visible sign of the miracles that come from *"doing what God is blessing"* is the clergy commitment to the conversation, meeting nearly every month for five years while maintaining focus on experiencing and sharing the encounter with the risen and living Christ. This is our faith; this is the Church! People who experience the miracle of Church are excited; diocesan staff responds differently; clergy and lay are more engaged in the communal life. After three years at the table in the communal gathering, the clergy defined their purpose and guide to future actions:

> *MISSION IN MOTION is a grassroots effort of several predominately African-American parishes in the Archdiocese of Washington and their pastors working in collaboration across deanery lines to strengthen the Catholic identity of our*

parishioners and to empower and equip them to embrace and carry out the work of the New Evangelization in our local communities.

Through my ten years of community organizing and several years of communal gatherings with clergy, the same question constantly resurfaces: How can we continue to meet and improve on the accomplishment of the Church's mission? The answer is to practice the "art of accompaniment" as described by Pope Francis. This practice is the focus of ecclesial movements in our Church, actions which are both "Catholic" and "catholic." The answer is simple and embodied in these inspired words: "They devoted themselves to the apostles' teaching and fellowship, to the breaking of bread and the prayers" (Acts 2:42).

I have said, *"The joy is in the action,"* which is the practice of the "art of accompaniment." What follows is the answer to the clergy questions about how to continue the Acts 2:42 conversation and improve on mission accomplishment. Each time the clergy convene in a communal gathering, clergy and lay leaders walk out of the meeting energized and with renewed focus on the mission. What follows is one deacon's prescription about how to continue the conversation. I invite you to read on if you want to experience the joy.

Timothy E. Tilghman
Washington, D.C.
The Year of Mercy

Someone good at accompaniment does not give in to frustrations or fears. He or she invites others to let themselves be healed, to take up their mat, and embrace the cross, leave all behind and go forth ever anew to proclaim the Gospel.

Holy Father Francis, *EG* #172

Accompaniment begins with a conversation, because folk simply won't walk with people they do not know. When I told my father that I planned to work as a community organizer, he told me "Timothy, when you tell people you want to know what *they* want to do, they will be suspicious, and when you stop to listen to their answers they will be doubly surprised because rarely do people get asked what they want to do by people who will help them do it." My father, the old union organizer, was a prophet. To a person, most folk responded just as my father said they would. When you stop and listen, everyone owns what comes next.

As I listened to pastors in communal gatherings and individual meetings, questions surfaced with the main questions being *"who?"* and *"how?"* The biggest discovery I have made from my organizing is that people want to act, but they want to act on what they believe. As my father said, however, "…rarely do people get asked what they want to do." If you get to know folk and listen to them, they will tell you what they want to do. And if you are willing to walk with them, they will do what they say. This is what I am calling "going to the well"—the people of God getting what they need to do God's work. This is what Jesus did with the Samaritan woman. If you want results like Jesus got from his conversation with her, do as Jesus did in their encounter.

Initiating a conversation with her about a drink of water, Jesus helped the woman answer not only the *"who?"* but also the *"how?"* The Samaritan woman knew "what" to do with the "who" and the "how," and she did it with great enthusiasm and spectacular results.

There are six facilitated conversations outlined in this booklet: ***Introduction to the Encounter, The First Encounter, The Leader, The Team, The Ideal Parishioner,*** and ***The Culture.*** Walk through the conversations with groups of leaders. The *"who?"* and *"how?"* will emerge, and people will take action on the "what" consistent with the faith we preach and model.

Conversation is best when followed by focused questions to stimulate sharing and introspection as individuals and as community. If you are honest in your conversations, especially the exploration of the questions, you will find answers that lead to specific, concrete actions. The organizing axiom still applies: "The joy is in the action." Read on only if you want to experience the joy! Starting the conversations moves us from talking to walking.

The essentials for Christians in these six conversations:

- Be open to Christ in the people you meet.
- Learn to share the essence of the encounters with your team as you prepare leaders.
- Determine priority actions from the six conversations.
- Conduct a parish census, internal then external, based on the encounter with the Samaritan woman at the well; modify actions based on census results.

⁙ ⁙ ⁙ ⁙ ⁙

CONVERSATION #1
REVELATION: THE INVITATION TO ENCOUNTER

This witness comforts and sustains me in my own effort to overcome selfishness and to give more fully of myself.

Holy Father Francis, *EG* #76

⁙ ⁙ ⁙ ⁙ ⁙

People are still coming to church, looking for the Christ our Holy Father met, the one who comforts and sustains the lonely, lost, and disinherited. These are the restless souls that Saint Augustine spoke of nearly 1,700 years ago. Too often they come into our midst looking for Christ and find bad news and cold, cautious people when they come to our parishes. We are witnesses, but what are we telling the folk in search of the comfort Christ offers?

In October 2012, Father Maurice Nutt preached from the Gospel of Mark at the closing Mass for the Annual East of the River Revival in Washington, D.C. There was a man, Fr. Nutt said, who approached Jesus out of frustration. When Jesus inquired about the man's frustration, he responds, "Teacher, I brought you my son; he has a spirit that makes him unable to speak…. I asked your disciples to cast it out, but they could not do so" (Mark 9:17-18). These disciples Mark describes are the folk people meet when they get to church. Father Nutt's message—we, the disciples of this day, could not get the demons out. The gospel is the truth that transcends time. Folk are coming to our parishes looking for someone who greets them as our Holy Father Francis does and they are frequently disappointed. Folk want community; we give bureaucracy.

Who is our Holy Father talking about? Folk that we meet in Mark's gospel: "Then some people came, bringing to him a paralyzed man, carried by four of them. And when they could not bring him to Jesus because of the crowd, they removed the roof above him…" (Mark 2:3-4). Yes! The crowd was too big, and the door was blocked, but four men were not deterred, they found the path of hope and carried their paralyzed brother to Christ. The neighborhoods surrounding our parishes are full of paralyzed people. Many of these folk are excited about our Holy Father's witness.

Pope Francis will not meet them in person, but our parishioners can. What will our people do—present the good news or the bad news? The answer is in the Gospel. Are we getting it right at your parish?

The New Evangelization speaks of the people who got it right with these words: "They devoted themselves to the apostles' teaching and fellowship, to the breaking of bread and the prayers" (Act 2:42). Our parishes are full of people whose actions are chronicled in Mark's gospel—the disciples who are dodging the demons as well as those who are aware of, but undeterred by, the bad news. Instead, they continue to take people to Christ.

The whole world sees the Pope—washing the feet of women, riding the metro train to work, meeting people at the gate to the Vatican, admitting to being a sinner, and asking "Who am I to judge others?" Non-Catholic or lapsed Catholics are moved by his actions and looking at the parish in their neighborhood, wondering if neighborhood Catholics are dodging demons and being ruled by doubt or overcoming demons and saving through hope.

When Jesus saw their faith, he said to the paralytic, "Son, your sins are forgiven" (Mark 2:5). As the doubters continued to doubt, Jesus forgave the sins of the paralytic and took care of his physical ailments too. This is our faith. Is this what we present when we meet people in the neighborhood?

The Scripture

Read Mark 2:1-12; 9:14-29, Acts 2:14-24.

＊ ＊ ＊ ＊ ＊

This witness comforts and sustains me in my own effort to overcome selfishness and to give more fully of myself.

Holy Father Francis, *EG* #76

God addresses man as a master his servant; God asks a question; man hearing God answers by faith and obedience. The fact and content of this communication are called revelation.

R. Latourelle, SJ, *Theology of Revelation*, p. 21

＊ ＊ ＊ ＊ ＊

The Questions

1. When did you encounter Christ? What did you do after the encounter?

2. If you cannot name the demons, you cannot remove the demons. What demons are present in your parish community? In the surrounding neighborhood?

Genuine spiritual accompaniment always begins and flourishes in the context of service to the mission of evangelization.

Holy Father Francis, EG #173

It is the encounter! The father whose son was possessed by the mute spirit (Mark 9:17-18) came to the disciples to get the demons out. The family trying to get rid of demons is still knocking on our parish doors today. They often meet the same old disciples, the ones who could not get the demons out. These disciples are so engaged in their own lives that they are unaware or afraid of the one who knocks. We must figure out how to accompany those who knock and walk in before we take the Church into the streets as the foursome did to share the encounter with the paralytic (cf. Mark 2:1-12).

Thirsty people with demons in their lives are looking for the well. That's why folk are attracted to Pope Francis. Our Holy Father exemplifies the encounter with the thirsty one, as told in the story of the Samaritan woman at the well (John 4:1-42). "*We can touch them where they are and help them to believe,*" as Earth, Wind & Fire says in their 1970's hit, "Touch the World." Many people saw the Holy Father in the media and then walked into a parish looking for folk like him. We told them to "see the Evangelization Committee" or "the deacon will get back to you," which is like sending the thirsty person into the desert. The next week we say, "Where is that woman who came in looking for a drink? We haven't seen her for a while. She must not have been that thirsty." *Real* accompaniment, the kind Father Francis is calling for, begins when whoever sees the thirsty woman offers her a drink of living water instead of sending her into the desert of parish bureaucracy. So what should happen when someone goes to the well in our parishes?

The thirsty are often uncomfortable, quiet, and different, especially when they come to the sanctuary. The Samaritan woman was different from the folk who would normally gather around the well. In fact, she waited until the off hours before going to fill her jar. Yet she found what she was looking for when she went to the well that day. Jesus was there, anticipating her presence and ready to accompany her on her spiritual journey. He was serving living water to quench her thirst for truth and meaning. So what did Jesus do with her?

- *Jesus was deliberate and intentional* in meeting her at her need—at the well, at the time when the "not so nice (un-churched)" appear.
- *Jesus initiated* the conversation and got some interesting responses—"Why is a Jew talking to me? I am 'different'" (i.e., a quiet,

uncomfortable, different woman, and a Samaritan at that).

- ***Jesus was inquisitive without condemning*** and found some common ground; Jacob, our father in faith, who provided the well, became the focus of the discussion.
- Jesus spoke of the living water in the Jacob conversation—something that was of interest to the woman. The woman who was different stayed in the conversation because ***Jesus listened and spoke to her interests***.
- Finally, ***Jesus had something to offer*** that was universally good, his relationship with the Father, and he could articulate what he had in her language.

This is the New Evangelization. The four men who carried the paralytic (Mark 2) had something to offer; Jesus was ready before he got to the well and knew something of the folk he would meet. Look at what happened to the paralytic. Look at how the Samaritan woman responded. Accompaniment, the essence of encounter, elicits a specific, tangible, concrete response. This is what should be happening when new folk come for a drink, but is it what happens at your parish or your house?

The Scripture
Read John 4:1-42.

Genuine spiritual accompaniment always begins and flourishes in the context of service to the mission of evangelization.

Holy Father Francis, *EG* #173

When we meet them at their need...we can touch them where they are.

Earth, Wind & Fire, "Touch the World"

The Questions

1. What can you share with the person who meets you on your turf or on the church grounds?

2. How do you first respond when thirsty folk show up. Do you engage them in the way that Jesus engaged the Samaritan woman at the well?

CONVERSATION #3
LEADER IN THE ENCOUNTER

Paul's relationship with Timothy and Titus provides an example of this accompaniment and formation which takes place in the midst of apostolic activity.

Holy Father Francis, *EG* #173

As you can see with Jesus' encounter with the Samaritan woman, leaders are deliberate and intentional initiators, inquisitive without being intrusive or judgmental, and extraordinary listeners. The conversation at the well was all about the Samaritan woman and, hearing all the bad, Jesus consistently sought the good, and he found it in the woman. Jesus took the first action of a leader: Leaders love! You must go to the well to drink yourself before you can give the living water to others.

The leader must first visit Jesus at the well before he or she is prepared for accompaniment. The big questions remain, *"Who?"* and *"How?"* As M. Scott Peck says in *The Road Less Traveled*, the answer to the first question is: "I have said the object of genuine love must be a person, since only people have spirits capable of growth." Clergy and those who pray the community prayers of the Church reflect on the answer to the second question in Sirach 39:1-10. This poetic text gives us what it takes to be prepared to meet the thirsty one by first remembering that we are thirsty, too. We want the best, so we strive to give the best. Timothy and Titus were good evangelists because Paul loved them. What are you doing to practice the art of accompaniment?

Read Sirach 39:1-10, then take a moment to revisit Jesus' encounter with the Samaritan woman. Jesus meets the Samaritan woman where she is, takes the initiative in the encounter, and listens very intently. After the exchange about the woman having multiple husbands, a usual conversation stopper, Jesus keeps the woman engaged. Hearing the worst but seeking the best is what accompaniment is all about: no judgment, just listening with love!

What about our encounter with a new person? In our talk with someone, often the conversation moves to "will you join my ministry or organization?" or even "will you buy a ticket to my fundraiser?" It is all about you and nothing about them! This is taking, not giving, the living water. Does this sound like your parish or your ministry? Perhaps someone did this to you, and now you are doing it to others.

"Come and see a man who told me everything I have ever done! He cannot be the Messiah, can he?" (John 4:29). This is the Samaritan woman's response to her encounter. Jesus listened, judged nothing, and offered everything. The woman's response was to invite everyone she knew to meet the man who knew everything about her. Peck continues with, "The genuine lover always respects and even encourages this separateness and the unique individuality of the be-loved." Paul was patient with Timothy and Titus and gave them the freedom to grow and choose a course of action in their ministry. Jesus, Paul, and our present Pope Francis have a commanding presence that moves people without telling them what to do.

How often do we present this commanding presence to the new or unknown person who comes to the parish? If this is not the experience of the new or unknown person, we have work to do as leaders.

The Scripture

Read Sirach 39:1-10 and John 1:1-42

Paul's relationship with Timothy and Titus provides an example of this accompaniment and formation which takes place in the midst of apostolic activity.

Holy Father Francis, *EG* #173

The first aspect is that I am a Christian; the second, that I am a leader. I am a Christian for my own sake, whereas I am a leader for your sake; the fact that I am a Christian is to my own advantage, but I am a leader for your advantage.

Saint Augustine of Hippo, from the beginning of a sermon on being pastors

1. Have you ever experienced an encounter like the Samaritan woman did at the well? How have you encountered the living Christ through a person that loved you? Describe what happened.

2. Can you tell a story about a person or persons who influenced your life in the Church? Do so now.

※ ※ ※ ※ ※

CONVERSATION #4
THE TEAM, PARTNERS IN ACCOMPANIMENT

All Christians, their pastors included, are called to show concern for the building of a better world.

Holy Father Francis, *EG* #183

※ ※ ※ ※ ※

Paul picked Timothy and Titus and others to do the work of the Church. This tradition goes back to the day of Moses, who selected Joshua and gave these instructions: "Choose some men for us and go out, fight with Amalek. Tomorrow I will stand on the top of the hill with the staff of God in my hand" (Exodus 17:9). During the fight with Amalek, we see that "Moses' hands grew weary; so they took a stone and put it under him, and he sat on it. Aaron and Hur held up his hands, one on one side, and the other on the other side; so his hands were steady until the sun set" (Exodus 17:12). Moses had folk to accompany him and even hold him up.

Today's pastor is engaged in protracted battles with the secular world, and he is often the only one in the rectory. The pastor's first inclination and seemingly easy solution—"I will do this myself; I can handle this." Knowing that today's Moses would fall into this trap, the Lord said to him: "Write this as a reminder in a book and recite it in the hearing of Joshua: I will utterly blot out the remembrance of Amalek from under heaven" (Exodus 17:14). Of course, today pastors always tell somebody to find the right folk to do evangelization, but if they don't have a plan, they retreat to the familiar *"I will do this myself"* routine. If it is done as the Lord instructed, however, pastors find themselves some Aarons and Hurs to help.

Yet the saga continues with the *"I don't have time with the funerals, bible study, marriage prep, meetings, and the stuff from the bishop's office"* lament from the pastor working solo. The answer is found in the Word of God. After prevailing against Amalek and documenting the keys to success, Moses then went back at it alone and went whining to his father-in-law, who said to him: "You will surely wear yourself out, both you and these people with you. For the task is too heavy for you; you cannot do it alone" (Exodus 18:18). Many ministry leaders emulate the behavior of their pastors—whining and doing it alone. But perhaps not at your parish—right?

We are striving to be like Jesus, so why don't we approach our ministry in the way he did? Jesus probably didn't read Sun Tzu's reasons for failure in his book, *The Art of War*, which included "Failure to use picked men." But before he embarked on his public ministry, Jesus picked twelve men, along with his mother and a few key women, to launch his revolution. He didn't go to the local university or the Sanhedrin; he went into the street and into the homes of sinners. Peter, the fisherman with the dirty hands who engaged his mouth before engaging his mind and who always acted on impulse was among those. Peter turned out to be a great leader, as did Paul, another follower with a lot of flaws, like, say, persecuting the early Christians! We are still marveling at their work today. So, just pick a few people from your parish, train them, and see what God has in store. Let them be blessed and grow by doing the Lord's work as Peter and Paul did.

Here is the invitation. How about suspending judgment and revisiting Exodus 17 and 18? Then approach public ministry as Moses, Jesus, Peter, and Paul did. The African-American spiritual says, "Try Christ; he'll make it better!" Don't lament. Just try it out in a communal gathering. Take Jethro's advice. Save yourself, empower your parishioners, and start building the better world.

Read Exodus 17:8-15; 18:13-27

❋ ❋ ❋ ❋ ❋

All Christians, their pastors included, are called to show concern for the building of a better world.

Holy Father Francis, *EG* #183

"... if you give people a thorough understanding of what it is that confronts them, and the basic causes that produce it, they'll create their own program, and when the people create a program, you get action."

Malcolm X, at the Audubon Theater

❋ ❋ ❋ ❋ ❋

The Questions

1. Revisit Moses' prescription for success in Exodus 17 and 18. Is this your parish experience? If not, why? Who is holding up trying this method?

2. Who and where are the able and God-fearing men and women in your parish to be set over groups of thousands, hundreds, fifties, and tens? Start naming them and approaching them.

The kerygma has a clear social content: at the heart of the Gospel is life in community and engagement with others.

Holy Father Francis, *EG* #177

The parish is the place where the engagement with the other takes place. The heart of the engagement, then, is the parishioner's experience of encounter. You cannot give what you do not have, so the ideal parishioner must experience and then share. But share with whom? Parishioners share with other parishioners; that is part of Holy Father Francis' concept of accompaniment. Since the Church still defines a parishioner as anyone created in God's image and likeness who lives in the geographic boundary of parish, that ideal parishioner has a plethora of opportunities to be, as the pope says, *"at the heart of the Gospel."*

Now let's be honest. Some of us are challenged to engage the person sitting with us in the pew. Imagine what it would take to see and engage the person who lives or works in our community as the focus of our accompaniment! Jesus met the Samaritan woman at the well, but that was business as usual for one who sought out tax collectors and prostitutes—not to criticize or patronize but to engage and encounter. Jesus encountered as he walked and sat with people in the neighborhood, but we drive to church and drive through the neighborhood. Jesus is the ideal, and I am not Jesus, so what about me? How can I engage others?

If you cannot do it as good as Jesus, follow his mother's example:

- *Mary was attentive* to the need of her neighbor, a fellow parishioner at the wedding at Cana (John 2:1-12).
- *She saw, she engaged, and without fanfare she introduced* the groom's people to Jesus. And the celebration continued.
- Focused on the needs of the other, *Mary walked* to Elizabeth's house (Luke 1:39-56) to see for herself if the news was true and to offer assistance, just as Jesus would later do.
- There were only parishioners in Mary's world. *Mary was aware of them* and *aware of her call to meet them* where they were, going to them, if that's what it took.

"But Mary treasured all these words and pondered them in her heart" (Luke 2:19). The ideal parishioner does three things with humility: observes life in the community, responds to the need he or she finds there, and, when the one in need of encounter is not where the parishioner is, the parishioner seeks out and serves that person wherever. The perfect disciple knows Jesus and brings Jesus to others. The object of the ideal parishioner's love experiences the personal encounter with the servant Jesus. The object of love responds with love and respect. Observe, seek, act... and reflect after sharing!

Mary is the model leader, the ideal parishioner, and the master in the art of accompaniment. Leaders love as Mary did. But what does that mean today, for me, at my parish and in my neighborhood? Loving means meeting the un-churched on their turf and being fully present to them. Loving means making God real to a high school student who is not just non-Catholic but not even vaguely familiar with the church. This lost, lonely, and suffering "parishioner" is still looking to get the demons out in order to tap the good within. Mary did not "drive by." Mary looked, listened, and gave of herself as the circumstances dictated. What about you?

* * * * *

The Scripture
Read Exodus Luke 1:39-56; John 2:1-12

* * * * *

The kerygma has a clear social content: at the heart of the Gospel is life in community and engagement with others.

Holy Father Francis, *EG* #177

When he saw the crowds, he had compassion for them....

Matthew 9: 36

■ ■ ■ ■ ■

The Questions

1. Have you met the ideal parishioner? What did he or she do that held your attention? Did you proposition him or her into evangelization?

2. Where would your ideal parishioner meet those in need who come into your parish or live or work in your community?

■ ■ ■ ■ ■

Church neighborhood?
- neighborhood
- Humane Society

41

Growth in justice requires more than economic growth, while presupposing such growth: it requires decisions, programs, mechanisms, and processes specifically geared to a better distribution of income, the creation of sources of employment, and an integral promotion of the poor which goes beyond a simple welfare mentality.

Holy Father Francis, *EG* #204

Justice is love in action. Loves equals charity. Charity begins at home. For the one who is suffering, and especially for us, this is our Church: the parish. Old folk remember this "local church," where "ma'am" and "sir" were common titles for elders, adults assumed responsibility for every child in the congregation, and church values permeated the neighborhood. The church about which our Holy Father speaks is just a new application of the old-time religion our elders remember. The characteristics of this Church come from the Vatican II *Decree on the Apostolate of the Laity.* The numbers below correspond to articles in that Vatican II decree. There are four characteristics of the parish, which is the Church in action:

- ***Church People and Their Associations.*** Our faith, which we believe and practice, must work in our everyday life. Organizations have purpose beyond social gatherings. If it is old and broken, we are called to change it. Just because it worked for the Knights of Columbus for thirty years does not mean we should use it to engage the youth. The Body of Christ is adaptable, dynamic, and—like Christ—always new (#19).
- ***Commitment to Public Action.*** Catholics versed in politics, as should be the case, should not hesitate to enter public life; they can work for the common good and prepare the way for the Gospel (#14). What should we consider when we act for the common good? Personal and family values, culture, economic interests, the trades and professions, political institutions, international relations, and so on… (#7). The charge to permeate the temporal order is a mandate to take the faith into every public institution.
- ***Model Public Institution.*** Today's local church is God's perfect love in action. She sees in her neighbors the image of God, in which all of humanity is created. Out of love, the demands of justice much be satisfied; what is already due in justice is not to be offered as a gift in charity (#8). As women are assuming expanded roles in society, their participation in the life of the church should also grow (#9).

As such, all parishioners are part of the solution to church and world problems and committed to the salvation of all. Responsibility extends beyond the parish and diocese and includes ensuring human rights in civic legislation (#10).

- *The Teaching Institution.* Through its commitment to Catholic education, parishes help create the middle class. Even when Catholic schools close, the commitment remains working through the family as the vital cell of society. Parishes foster vocations, defining the values for all those who are in public life, while encouraging those who are called to ministry in the religious life, too (#11). Finally, the parish sets the example for behavior in the home, professional, and social life through grounding all in faith and doctrine (#29).

The big question is: Would folk in the neighborhood describe your parish this way?

※ ※ ※ ※ ※

Read Acts 1:13-14; 2:5-13; 2:37-41

☒ ☒ ☒ ☒ ☒

Growth in justice requires more than economic growth, while presupposing such growth: it requires decisions, programs, mechanisms, and processes specifically geared to a better distribution of income, the creation of sources of employment, and an integral promotion of the poor which goes beyond a simple welfare mentality.

Holy Father Francis, EG #204

They devoted themselves to the apostles' teaching and fellowship, to the breaking of bread and the prayers.

Acts 2:42

☒ ☒ ☒ ☒ ☒

The Questions

1. Are your parish organizations inviting, welcoming, real, and relevant? Why or why not? Give some examples.

2. How does your parish positively impact the quality of life for its members and the surrounding community? How could it do it better?

PART #2
THE RIGHT PRIORITIES

God attracts us by taking into account the complex interweaving of personal relationships entailed in the life of a human community. This people which God has chosen and called is the Church.

Holy Father Francis, EG #113

This is all about building the Church at the local level. The Church is a community of people in relationship that act in concert. It is the Body of Christ, our God acting in the world to transform lives. If committed to action that transforms, do as the Samaritan woman did—go to the well to drink the living water. Jesus Christ is the living water, the eternal thirst quencher who always has more in the well. You cannot go to this well too often.

Going to the well to build community always results in transformation, action that produces real tangible results. The Samaritan woman went to the well looking for something and found the Messiah (John 4:26), witnessed to the discovery that transformed her life (John 4:39), and prompted many others to discover what comes from walking with the Messiah (John 4:42). This pattern repeats in the Acts of the Apostles with witnesses who met the Christ

(Acts 1:8), shared the communal life (Acts 1:14), testified on a large scale (Acts 2:8-11), and inspired others to action (Acts 2:41-42).

Here is an example of how all this happens at the local level. Building Our Lady of Perpetual Help School at my parish in D.C. was a tangible result of transforming action. Parishioners, largely engaged in domestic work around Washington, D.C., transformed the school from a single classroom in the basement of the old church to a two-campus primary school with more than 600 students. These parishioners were also engaged in the Civil Rights movement in the United States. It was these relationships, communal life, and action by those of one accord that transformed. This was and is the Church, and the church.

Building this local church is the goal of our focused conversations, a church where people drink the living water, where Jesus is "the way, and the truth, and the life" (John 14:6). The church acts in the world for the good of those sharing the communal life and others in the community. Staying in the conversation continually exposes the parish to the depth of God's love by helping members discover and act in the world with their gifts. The priorities to sustain the conversations are:

- *POWER:* using gifts for the good of self and others is the imperative.
- *RELATIONSHIPS:* you cannot work with people until you know them.
- *COMMUNAL LIFE:* preserve the individual

identity but act on one accord in the world.
- **LEADERS:** loving and being loved so that gifts emerge and get used for the right things.
- **WALKING:** moving around to meet leaders as Jesus did and staying with them.
- **SPIRITUALITY:** being still to know God by prayer, reflection, and focus on the agenda.
- **REFLECTION:** God took the seventh day to examine his work; why not do as he did?

PRIORITY #1
POWER

Nobody can go off to battle unless he is fully convinced of victory beforehand. If we start without confidence, we have already lost half the battle and we bury our talents.

Holy Father Francis, *EG* #87

Since its beginning, our Church has endured persecution and persevered to build the part of the God's kingdom. How did the Church wield power in the midst of persecution? Jesus often said to his disciples, "…your faith has made you well" (Mark 5:34; 10:52).

My home parish, Our Lady of Perpetual Help

Church, celebrates the history of the parish's founding in 1920 on the fourth Sunday in June. Elders back then petitioned Cardinal Gibbons to build their own parish so that Negroes (as they were called then) and all others in the neighborhood could experience the dignity of human life that is at the core of Catholic social teaching. Convinced of victory beforehand, men and women of faith walked to the site of the new parish in the summer of 1920. A faith community comprised largely of domestic workers, found the wherewithal to build a church. Men from the parish provided construction labor after working full days at other jobs. This is our faith!

At the parish's eighty-fifth anniversary, the community celebrated a bittersweet moment with the closing of Our Lady of Perpetual Help School. That evening, my brother, Charles, recounted the school's history. In the 1940s, when Charles attended the one-room school in the basement of the old church, he recalled the adult conversation he heard about the need for a new and larger school to serve the needs of more youth in the neighborhood. "For which of you, intending to build a tower, does not first sit down and estimate the cost, to see whether he has enough to complete it" (Luke 14:28). Counting the cost as they did in 1920, this next generation of this faith community of domestic workers increased its tithes, regularly adding nickels, dimes, and quarters to their weekly contributions. In 1957, the community celebrated the opening of a new school, which for many years was among the largest primary schools in the Archdiocese of Washington.

Many of the students from this school crossed the river to integrate schools, acting on Archbishop O'Boyle's mandate to integrate Catholic parishes and schools in the Archdiocese six years before Brown v. Board of Education. Many of these students and their parents joined Dr. Martin Luther King, Jr., for the August 1963 March on Washington, one of the greatest demonstrations of the Church's power in the history of the United States.

What's the point? With faith and vision, our parish communities have power to transform. This is true not only at Our Lady of Perpetual Help but in every parish where members commit to live the faith. Jesus intervened in the world: "...to serve and to give his life as a ransom for many" (Matthew 20:28). We are the Body of Christ, the domestic workers who built a parish and a school, who fought the fight for integration and marched on Washington. We are "the salt of the earth" (Matthew 5: 13). By faith we have the power to transform. Victory is assured if we have the confidence to act on our faith. Do we have the courage to use this power in the world today? Many lives depend on the way we answer this question.

Being a Christian is not the result of an ethical choice or a lofty idea, but the encounter with an event, a person, which gives life a new horizon and a decisive direction.

Holy Father Francis, *EG* #7

The story of Our Lady of Perpetual Help Church is unique to a particular community in the Archdiocese of Washington. There is a common element in the unique story of a parish and the local church. God was always in conversation with Abraham, Moses, and other patriarchs of the Church. There was no internet, fax, or cellphone, but parishes grew and thrived back in the day. How? Relationships! We build the Church in the same way the Lord did with Moses: "Thus the LORD used to speak to Moses face to face, as one speaks to a friend." (Exodus 33:11). Relations begin with those face-to-face conversations that include the following elements:

- *Hanging out:* People are impressed with our Holy Father. Why? Because of what they see and hear about his face-to-face meetings with others. These same people are walking into our parishes, looking for a similar personal encounter, a projection of our Holy Father. They cannot relate to a projection; it is real people who make the encounter and cement the relationship. It is more than simply hanging out together. We must be *with* them!

- *Discovery:* Projections are a series of assumptions, assumptions to be checked out in a real conversation about shared experiences, thoughts, and hopes. Moses cemented the relationship with the Lord and others through face-to-face conversations where a commitment to action was revealed. There are two reasons that relationships fail: attempting to relate to a projection or unwillingness to stay in the conversation.
- *Talking:* I hear organizers like Mike Gecan of the Industrial Areas Foundation saying, "All relating is meeting." The relationship begins when we hear the thoughts, feelings, hopes, and ambitions of the other. If we don't listen, we cannot have a real conversation; the best talkers listen at least twice as long as they talk. The listener projects the sense that the conversation is about the "other" person.
- *Enlightenment:* We begin to feel good because we listened to the other person and know something about him or her. The real surprise is not what we learn about the other person, however, it is what we learn about ourselves because we were deliberate and intentional

in listening. When we make it to this level of enlightenment, learning is accelerated for us and for the other. When we all know more, we can all do more.

- ***Progression:*** We begin the accelerated growth process. We know, love, and see the best in the other; the other person grows as well. When we make it to this stage, the other becomes the best that he or she could be. When we discover the best in the other, we also see the best in ourselves.

Think for a moment. Abraham, Moses, Peter, and Paul did great things. Why? They stayed in the conversation with the Lord and then engaged in similar conversations with their brothers and sisters. There is no substitute for building relationships in this manner. It is simple: no relationships, no real power. This is the real work of the local church, the parish.

The parish is the presence of the Church in a given territory, an environment for hearing God's word, for growth in Christian life, for dialogue, proclamation, charitable outreach, worship, and celebration.

Holy Father Francis, *EG* #28

When speaking of the New Evangelization, Cardinal Donald Wuerl often referred to Acts 2:42: "They devoted themselves to the apostles' teaching and fellowship, to the breaking of bread and the prayers." This is the Church, the group of believers in prayer and dialogue about sharing their encounter with the risen and living Christ.

During the last twenty years, I've had three consistent and vivid experiences of this Church. The first is in the Cursillo movement, where every person that experiences the passion of a small group of Cursillistas is moved by the love shared in the group and with the powerful witness of the small community. Second, through Cursillo I joined a small group of four lay men who witnessed regularly to one another about living the faith. One of us married and the three others moved from the group to ordained ministry—two priests and me, the permanent deacon. Third and most recently, I have witnessed how the communal gathering of clergy involved in Mission in Motion has animated parishioners in and beyond their parishes. Each time clergy engaged lay people in a conversation about living the faith, new witnesses emerge from the laity in their presence.

Many in the world are looking for the vivid experiences of encounter with the risen and living Christ. Most folk will not have the chance for that direct relationship with Pope Francis, but they will have the chance to come to our parish, which is the Body of Christ practicing the art of accompaniment in a given territory. Folk are coming to our parishes, looking for community. They are seeking a small group of faithful lay men and women and clergy who embrace them through the presentation of word and sacrament. Anxious for the personal or community encounter, these folk often get a bulletin and a cold stare before dismissal. Of course, you are saying what most of us are saying: "This does not happen at my parish."

I will repeat something that Father Patrick Smith said to encourage his parishioners: "We have everything we need, everything God requires. I am primarily referring to you. Every gift, every skill, every virtue is here."

All these gifts already reside in every parish. The parish is called to be the Body of Christ in a given territory. It is not the individual or the group that causes the stranger to call our local church "home." It is the one Christ within us that is the attraction in this encounter. In our parishes, Father Patrick Smith says,

"Every gift, every skill, every virtue is here." We all strive to be the ideal parish, part of the Body of Christ that presents the gifts that come from God and also recognizes those gifts in the stranger or quiet one who comes into our community.

The parish is the beloved community for which lonely brothers and sisters hunger. We are called to be that beloved community that first welcomes, then comforts and nurtures.

PRIORITY #4
CHRISTIAN LEADERS

A proposal of goals without an adequate communal search for the means of achieving them will inevitably prove illusory.

Holy Father Francis, *EG* #33

Far too often, those we charge with building the community live in isolation. Pastors, pastoral associates, deacons, and other ministry leaders hold positions of responsibility with the (unjustified and unreasonable) expectation that they can and must do it all. This is not new. Moses started this way, too. When Moses got stuck, Jethro shared with him this timeless counsel on how to get things done:

> *But you should also look among all the people for able and God fearing men, trustworthy men who hate dishonest gain, and set them as officers over groups of thousands, of hundreds, of fifties and of tens. Let these men render decisions for the people in ordinary cases. More important cases they should refer to you.... You should also look for able men among all the people, men who fear God, are trustworthy, and hate dishonest gain; set such men over them as officers over thousands, hundreds, fifties, and tens. Let them sit as judges for the people at all times; let them bring every important case to you.... (Exodus 18:21-22).*

We religious professionals "should also look among all the people for able and God-fearing" people because they are the only means to achieve the goal of building our parishes. If building the Body of Christ is the ultimate goal, remember and apply this axiom from Msgr. Charles Pope: "Shepherds don't produce sheep. Sheep produce sheep!" After many missteps, Peter got it right and tells us: "...to tend the flock of God that is in your charge, exercising the oversight not under compulsion but willingly, as God would have you do it" (1 Peter 5:2). Jesus didn't embark on his public ministry until he picked the twelve. Let's all try doing it his way and pick the leaders in the flock that will help us achieve the ultimate goal. And we must pick the lay leaders first!

The important work of the shepherd is finding leaders in the flock. Surrounded by "Peters"—male and female, impulsive and imperfect, waiting for someone to do for them what Jesus did for Peter—we must look beyond their flaws and imperfections at the light of Christ within. Then these leaders need to work to magnify the light! M. Scott Peck best described the work of a leader in his book *The Road Less Traveled*, saying, "Leaders love!"

Peter made more than a few mistakes. His missteps are well-chronicled in Scripture. The Samaritan woman had six husbands, five "priors" plus one in the "current" relationship. Jesus loved Peter and the woman, acknowledging their flaws while continuing to walk with them. In time, Peter and the Samaritan woman became enthusiastic and courageous witnesses for the faith. Fully aware of the impact of the Good Shepherd's love, they brought others to the Body of Christ by the conviction of their witness (Revelation 12:11). Love is the engine that animates the witness. God IS love!

Jesus loved everyone. Jesus sought and chose the twelve from among those he loved and invested time in them. Imagine the time invested in Peter to prepare him to lead. Want a similar result? Find the "Peters" in among your sheep. Love, listen, and walk with them. Only then can you watch them bring the sheep into the one fold with the Good Shepherd, whose body is the Church as experienced on the local level.

Often it is better simply to slow down, to put aside our eagerness in order to see and listen to others, to stop rushing from one thing to another, and to remain with someone who has faltered along the way.

Holy Father Francis, *EG* #46

* * * * *

Canon 518 defines parish membership as "having a domicile or quasi-domicile in its boundaries...all persons in the territory belong to it." There is no mention of tithing, registration, Mass attendance, or receiving the sacraments. If you are human and live in the defined boundaries, you're in. Based on this canon, a law of the Catholic Church, we are often disconnected from our closest parish "members."

The commuter parish is prevalent in my archdiocese. Folk drive to church for Sunday Mass and an occasional weekday meeting. They then get out of the car in the church parking lot and never meet the people they pass along the way, people that by definition are their fellow parishioners. We unconsciously become drive-by Christians, becoming disconnected from those who are geographically close but spiritually distant from our parish community.

"My parish is different" is frequently the retort of

those who only get out of cars in the parking lot or the driveway at home. Parishes are in transition, of course, because people of means are mobile, and the unchurched are the largest segment of the parish community. But very often the mobile are moving in while the poor are being pushed out. Relationship-building only works when we can provide stability for the mobile and still walk with the poor.

What kind of Church do we need in the neighborhood in transition? In a July 2013 homily in his old neighborhood in Argentina, Pope Francis said:

> *We need a Church unafraid of going forth into their night. We need a Church capable of meeting them on their way. We need a Church capable of entering into their conversation. We need a Church able to dialogue with those disciples who, having left Jerusalem behind, are wandering aimlessly, alone, with their own disappointment, disillusioned by a Christianity now considered barren, fruitless soil, incapable of generating meaning.*

When we constantly talk about "THEM," it speaks volumes about "US." The main problem is not the crime, the bad schools, the poor folk, or the prevalence of the unchurched. The main problem is the drive-by Christian who is disconnected from and reluctant to meet the poor, the unchurched, and the mis-educated. At the end of the day, some of us identify "THEM" as the problem. We see "THEM" as isolated, different, and unknown because we are reluctant to invite

"THEM" to join "US." We don't slow down, listen, and meet "THEM." We see "THEM" and keep driving.

History proves that "WE" would be better off if "WE" knew another way. Jesus said, "I am the way, and the truth, and the life" (John 14: 6). Many of us remember a day when we walked to church, all adults intervened for the good of all children, and we spoke to everyone along the way. This is the local church at its best. Life was better not because folk were rich and technologically advanced but because we all stopped and drank the living water together. The big question is: Do we have the faith and courage to walk and share the way with one another?

* * * * *

PRIORITY #6
SPIRITUALITY

We only devote periods of quiet time to the things or the people whom we love, and here we are speaking of the God whom we love, a God who wishes to speak to us.

Holy Father Francis, EG #146

* * * * *

You can invite the Spirit or invite the chaos. One priest I know was hosting a meeting of local pastors and wanted to demonstrate genuine concern for each of his brother priests. He answered the door, made the coffee, and checked with his staff to make sure that they understood and practiced his definition of Christian hospitality. At the end of the meeting, the priest made an observation—"I think we need to have three elements every time we gather: PRAYER, SCRIPTURE REFLECTION, and *then* the AGENDA!" The priest first played the role of Martha, but then voiced his concern about missing her sister Mary's "better part" (Luke 10:42).We have to do both. Have you ever been to a meeting where participants were everywhere except centered in the Gospel and focused on the agenda? We all know that the best things in church are always preceded by prayer and scripture reflection. So why are our pastoral council or ministry meetings different from the best in the church? You've heard this saying: *"The road to hell is paved with good intentions."* My priest friend had good intentions, but the enemy of the best is often the good. Focused on good coffee, good hospitality, and good staff presentation, in the end he clamored for the essence (prayer, scripture reflection, and the agenda) during the evaluation of the day. Some days, we even miss the good, skipping even the coffee and hospitality and move immediately into "the negatives" of the agenda.

Pastors are like their members in many ways. Trained to preach and administer sacraments, they are often immersed in other details that affect the Church in the world. Leaders are often volunteers that come from the challenges of work-life and family into ministry meetings. When people come into a meeting from the world and are immediately immersed into the challenges of the world, the way of the world tends to dominate. You may have been to the meeting—whining, talk of what should have been and who didn't do what. At the end, the participants lost a couple of hours and got little if any water from the well. Before we go into any meeting, we should remember that Mary got the better part. When we start with the best, we get a better outcome; that is God's way.

"They devoted themselves to the apostles' teaching and fellowship, to the breaking of bread and the prayers" (Acts 2:42). The disciples gathered in the upper room to get away from the world and in touch with Christ, the Master Teacher. Prayer and scripture reflection set the stage for them to become Christ in the world. Ordinary people got extraordinary results in the world by starting with the best. Why not begin each communal gathering with prayer and reflection? Prayer and reflection usually bring us to listening, introspection, and centering on what is truly important. Kingdom-building action will always follow!

With prayer, scripture reflection, and then focused attention on the agenda, the object of the community's action does not see a group of people who are performing a task. They see the Church, which is God's presence and love at work in the world. If we start with God's love in mind, we will then do what God wants us to do.

The spirit of love which reigns in a family guides both mother and child in their conversations; therein they teach and learn, experience correction, and grow in appreciation of what is good.

Holy Father Francis, *EG* #139

⬚ ⬚ ⬚ ⬚ ⬚

I want to focus on organizing here. Organizers follow the Creator's lead, stopping and looking at the world to assess the effectiveness of their work. Organizing helped me to recognize the family about which Pope Francis speaks. Every member can be parent, child, teacher, or student, always giving and receiving in the spirit of the Creator. In the local Church, the communal gathering of clergy and my permanent deacon classmates are best at reflection when we do it in the spirit of the Creator.

"How different the man who devotes himself to the study of the Most High! He explores the wisdom of the men of old and occupies himself with the prophecies" (Sirach 39:1). The spirit of family that Pope Francis describes comes from the devotion to study the wisdom of the Creator. The prayer and scripture reflection in solitude, and especially in community, increase our awareness of God's grace within. The awareness of grace moves us towards action to discover and act on the truth. This is an invitation to pray and reflect in community on a regular basis. This is the experience of the upper room gathering with organizers, my deacon classmates, my Cursillo groups, and the gathering of clergy.

The true call to community is the call to reflection with brothers and sisters who are committed to act on their faith. When she became aware that I was moving in the direction of writing this book, Amy Vruno, my organizer colleague, gave me a book with this note inside the front cover:

> *The strength of your ministry has been and will continue to be that you know, in your heart, your mind, and your bones that Jesus' walk was with and among the people. Continue to walk with the people, especially those at the margins of society, but at the center of God's kingdom. You already know that is where God's best learning and teaching takes place.*

The strength of a community lies in its willingness to be deliberate and intentional about following the lead of the Creator in stopping and assessing the quality of its work. We must make a commitment to walk, to do real work, to risk, to go against the tide. The leaders of the Civil Rights movement did this —they met and had spirited discussions about what happened and the appropriate next steps. There was always healthy, positive tension. There was transformation of the individuals in the meetings, the object of their actions, and the world around them. This is our faith. This is our Church. You cannot experience the fullness of God's grace without stopping on the seventh day to assess before taking the next step.

I have yet to experience the fullness of God's grace, but I am most aware of being on that path when a colleague calls me to stop and reflect. When I stay in the conversation and in community, someone is going to challenge me to move through the adversity and take the next step to action and a deeper encounter. I can say this because of my experience with organizer colleagues, deacon classmates, my Cursillo community, and the communal gathering of clergy. The conversation is challenging, filled with tension, and at times disconcerting. If I am willing to endure the crucible of reflection, however, the enduring result is the joy of being part of the Creator's action in the world. There is no greater joy, but you must take the walk to experience this joy. My hope is that you want to experience real joy!

This people which God has chosen and called is the Church. Jesus did not tell the apostles to form an exclusive and elite group. He said: "Go and make disciples of all nations" (Matthew 28: 19).

Holy Father Francis, *EG* #113

❈ ❈ ❈ ❈ ❈

The personal invitation from one who is living his vocation in the larger community will make the conversations richer and the resulting mission-directed actions more fruitful. This section is dedicated to the persons, clergy and lay, who will extend the invitations to people from the community who will participate in the six focused conversations.

On April 22, 2015, I sat in the last communal gathering with clergy before sending this book to the publisher. Clergy were impressed with the fruit of their most recent evangelization effort, twenty-five youth and twenty catechists from five parishes committed to meet at a religious order's seminary for a pre-confirmation day of reflection the following weekend. The promise of twenty-five adolescents with catechists at a seminary for a day devoted to how to live their vocations made an indelible impression on the assembled clergy.

Based on the response, one of the pastors who was also on the diocesan seminary's faculty suggested a similar approach to priest vocations. He invited the six priests with him on April 22, 2015, to extend personal invitations to young men in their respective parish communities to a similar communal gathering to discuss vocations to the priesthood. Recalling their discernment experience, which included the personal invitation, the seven priests committed to extend the invitations and meet with the young men they were to invite before and after the communal gathering to discuss vocations.

At the April 22, 2015, meeting the priests and deacons in the communal gathering committed to some concrete mission-directed actions. Impressed with the results achieved by two catechists who were invited to plan the pre-confirmation day of reflection, priests committed to invite selected catechists to meet and discuss other ways to more constructively engage youth in the life of the local church and inviting young people to continued discipleship. A booklet, *Lend Your Voice to Christ*, was distributed at the meeting. One of the priests at the meeting commented on the booklet after the meeting. His summary of the book was that it was clear, concise, and compelling. In his twenty-five years of ordained ministry, however, he had never participated in a communal gathering to discuss what was in the content of the booklet.

The book's message was that the most critical element in a person's commitment to ordained ministry is a personal invitation to discern from another person who is already a living witness in their community. This is universally applicable. Over the last five years, each time the clergy have responded to a personal invitation or extended an invitation to act to a particular lay person in the church community, the results have far exceeded expectations of the clergy and the invited lay persons. Knowing the yield that comes from extending the personal invitations, those interested in accomplishing the mission of the Church should continue the conversations and focus on those they will invite to lead the mission-directed effort.

Everyone created in God's image and likeness is invited to be part of the Body of Christ. Our Holy Father reminds us that God has no exclusionary rule. When we look at the ministry of Jesus Christ we recall many times when he spoke to the masses before calling the disciples aside to go into greater depth about the mission. Anyone called to lead God's people has to look at at least three conversations: talking with the Father in prayer, conversing with the twelve (the potential leaders), and teaching the masses.

Moses spoke to the Lord before selecting Joshua and other leaders to engage Amalek (Exodus 17:9). Jesus selected the twelve and met with them repeatedly to prepare them for the mission ahead. Talking to the Father, intimate conversations with leaders, and teaching the masses are always necessary to accomplish the mission of the Church.

After creation, God consistently worked through his people to accomplish the mission through the ordained and other ministers charged to hear, nurture, and accompany the people called to be his own. The Lord's way has staying power. We suffer unnecessarily and experience an inordinate number of setbacks because we insist on doing it our way instead of following the Lord's way. Moses and Joshua picked men to lead the twelve tribes into the Promised Land; Jesus selected twelve before he embarked on his public ministry. Many clergy who are today's shepherds move immediately to the mission without first finding and nurturing their team as Moses and Jesus did. Then they feel isolated and overburdened, but they rarely reach out to a spiritually mature confidant as Moses did.

Feeling isolated and overburdened? Check and see if you are skipping one of the three conversations. There is only one task more difficult than picking the twelve; it is accomplishing the mission alone. The conversations, especially the one with the Father, are essential to accomplish the mission. Listening to the Spirit sent by the Father is at the heart of the conversation. Skip the first conversation; lose the battle. It is that simple. Jesus always went to the Father before he went to God's people; recall his prayer from John 17:20-21: "I do not pray for these only, but also for those who believe in me through their word, that they may all be one; even as you, Father, are in me, and I in you, that they also may be in us, so that the world may believe that you have sent me."

As you reflect on and prepare for the conversations, think about what Jesus did to prepare Peter. Peter did not "get it" on the first day, or in the first or second conversation. The Church stands today on Peter's body of work. To get similar results, take similar actions.

※ ※ ※ ※ ※

SPECIAL CONVERSATION #1
THE GOOD SHEPHERD AND ME

"Father, protect them in your name that you have given me, so that they may be one, as we are one."

John 17:11

※ ※ ※ ※ ※

The art of accompaniment, which is genuine love and relationship with the other, begins when we live as Jesus lived. In the Cursillo movement, leaders are consistently reminded to *"Talk to God about the other before talking to the other about God."* Jesus had a routine that is worth adopting; he spent time in community with the Father before engaging others, so that he always showed compassion for people.

What is your routine to prepare for engaging the people of God and inviting them to be the Church in the world surrounding the local church, the parish? In formation for ordination, we are told that the ones who lose focus are those who are not religious about the first conversation, the talk with the Father in prayer. When faced with the question about the quality of your prayer life, for example, be honest, because when people see you struggle it gives them permission to struggle as they persist in working the mission. This sets the stage for you to invite new leaders to assume a larger role in the mission. When the disengaged see the community of leaders who persevere in mission together, they will want a piece of the action because of the attraction of participating in the art of accompaniment. (Note that it is not just Catholics who are curious about and attracted to Pope Francis.)

In the conversation about leaders, I invited you to reflect on Sirach 39:1-10 in preparation to engage in a focused conversation about engaging the other as Jesus engaged the Samaritan woman at the well. As you reflect on Sirach here, I invite you to look in the mirror using this Scripture from the Common of Doctors. Consider what and how you study to stay mission-ready. Who is in your community of spiritually mature disciples? How often do you meet together to focus on your shared vision and mission? Finally, how does the quality and consistency of your communal prayer life help you attract other leaders? Recall John 10:14-16:

> *I am the good shepherd. I know my own and my own know me, just as the Father knows me and I know the Father. And I lay down my life for the sheep. I have other sheep that do not belong to*

this fold. I must bring them also, and they will listen to my voice. So there will be one flock, one shepherd.

Like it or not, you are the picture of the Good Shepherd in the parish community. The mission is accomplished when this picture is clear and bright. What must you do to make this word come to life in your parish community?

※ ※ ※ ※ ※

The Scriptures

Read John 14:12 and 15:15

※ ※ ※ ※ ※

The Questions

1. Do leaders sense they have the freedom to act on their vocation and mission because they know their Shepherd? If not, why not? What could you do to make it happen?

2. Do leaders see themselves as friends who can share with their Shepherd about their vocation and associated mission goals? If not, how can you invite them into such a relationship with you and with others on your team?

"I have other sheep that do not belong to this fold. I must bring them also, and they will listen to my voice. So there will be one flock, one shepherd."

John 10:16

＊ ＊ ＊ ＊

People who hunger to do the Lord's work in the neighborhood are not all in the pews. Think about the image of the Good Shepherd before engaging in the conversation about the role of a shepherd leader. Neighborhood elders, even those who do not regularly attend church or profess a strong belief in any organized religion, will remember Psalm 23 because many grew up in a day when public assemblies began with its proclamation and the pledge of allegiance. Tap into this memory; probe about parish and community members living this scripture; then engage in some introspection. Ask the question: How are you as pastor, parish priest, or ministry leader modeling the behavior of the Good Shepherd in living your call to action in the community?

After retreating to converse with the Father, the Good Shepherd invested much of his life in the midst of the sheep of his flock, the people of God. Often pastors, priests, and ministry leaders live in isolation from the people of God placed in their care. Why? Too much in the inbox, too many calls to the bishop's staff, and nagging repairs to the church buildings. It may be challenging to invite the people of God into the Shepherd's fold even under ideal circumstances. And, since you are like most in the business of inviting souls into the flock, your situation is probably less than ideal. Saint Peter had a charge for those called to shepherd the people of God. Remember: Peter is one of us in many ways—impulsive, imperfect, and mistake prone:

> *Now as an elder myself and a witness of the sufferings of Christ, as well as one who shares in the glory to be revealed, I exhort the elders among you to tend the flock of God that is in your charge, exercising the oversight, not under compulsion but willingly, as God would have you do it—not for sordid gain but eagerly. Do not lord it over those in your charge, but be examples to the flock. And when the chief shepherd appears, you will win the crown of glory that never fades away (1 Peter 5:1-4).*

You are one of the spiritually mature elders. Saint Peter knew the original Good Shepherd, and after some trial and error, witnessed with great authority and passion so that many joined the one flock. Now that you know the Good Shepherd, how are you at modeling his behaviors and his love? Explore the Scriptures and questions on the next page.

Read Psalm 23 and 1 Peter 5:1-4.

▨ ▨ ▨ ▨ ▨

The Questions

1. What interferes with your loving God's people the way that the Good Shepherd loves you? How can you begin to overcome those things?

2. What one thing could you do to make the people in your care more aware of the Good Shepherd's presence in their midst? How could you role-model this?

▨ ▨ ▨ ▨ ▨

*"Peace be with you. As the Father has sent me,
so I send you."*

John 20:21

※ ※ ※ ※ ※

You are working hard to live John's gospel, noting that Jesus used these words when he charged the disciples to go forth and build the Church. There is something unique about the community you serve, but there is something you may have in common with many of your colleagues—that is, not enough lay people engaged in the work of the parish. Parish priests are often overworked, under-staffed, and isolated. And, when you utter Jesus' words to your would be disciples, few if any respond. Jesus went to the well to bring others into his flock of willing workers. Remember what happened when he met the Samaritan woman? How many parishioners do you meet where they are—at the well? And, how many respond to you as the Samaritan woman did after her encounter with Jesus?

You are not the first one to be overburdened and short of willing workers, and more money to hire them is not the first solution. The challenge of getting folk to move with you predates Moses' lament and Jethro's response. Help comes from the spiritually mature who share the communal life with you; they can be fellow clergy, religious, or lay people. Moses prevailed in the battle with Amalek because he picked Joshua and allowed Aaron and Hur to support his arms during the battle. He then went home, however, and returned to business as usual before whining to his father-in-law about too much work and no assistance. Moses lamented to his father-in-law, and Jethro responded in these words from Exodus 18:17-22:

"What you are doing is not good. You will surely wear yourself out, both you and these people with you. For the task is too heavy for you; you cannot do it alone. Now listen to me. I will give you counsel, and God be with you! You should represent the people before God, and you should bring their cases before God; teach them the statutes and instructions and make known to them the way they are to go and the things they are to do. You should also look for able men among all the people, men who fear God, are trustworthy, and hate dishonest gain; set such men over them as officers over thousands, hundreds, fifties, and tens. Let them sit as judges for the people at all times; let them bring every important case to you, but decide every minor case themselves. So it will be easier for you, and they will bear the burden with you."

What would happen at your parish or in particular ministries if you or the ministry leader took Jethro's advice or followed the example of Jesus' meeting with the Samaritan woman at the well? Accompaniment or personal contact, the conversation, and requests to act on God's call will engage potential leaders. Will you make the initial contact?

❊ ❊ ❊ ❊ ❊

The Scriptures

Read Exodus 17:8-15; 18:13-27.

❊ ❊ ❊ ❊ ❊

The Questions

1. Who in your flock has passion to act on their faith in a ministry? Name them. If you cannot, then what is your strategy to find them?

2. What burdens do you have at present that could be lifted by developing a leader in your flock? Do it.

❊ ❊ ❊ ❊ ❊

SPECIAL CONVERSATION #4
CONTINUING THE CONVERSATION,
THE NEXT CHAPTER OF ACTS

"I do not call you servants any longer, because the servant does not know what the master is doing; but I have called you friends, because I have made known to you everything that I have heard from my Father."

John 15:15

If our goal is to achieve a different outcome, we must behave in a different way. I caught a glimpse of that different way in my work as a community organizer. Asking people what they believe and inviting them to act on that articulated faith in their public lives, organizers saw people transform neighborhoods and move communities to change for the betterment of all. The best picture of the different way in recent U.S. history is the Civil Rights movement, which is a picture of the Church at its best. Black and White, rich and poor, immigrant and native born, conservative and liberal, religious and atheist came together around a common definition of the truth and took decisive action. A son of the south championed voting rights and our nation and the world changed.

That change had a public face, a young pastor named Martin Luther King, Jr. Starting conversations in a small church in Montgomery, Alabama, Dr. King found himself in conversations well beyond his congregation. King did not do it by himself; he was constantly engaged in conversations with people of faith. Our Holy Father Francis echoes themes from Vatican II in his encyclical *The Joy of the Gospel*, reintroducing the call for today's pastors to be in conversation with the flock through the "art of accompaniment." Clergy and lay people today are restless as they were during the Civil Rights movement and Vatican II. The restless souls cannot find peace without being in conversation, a conversation which starts with pastors and other clergy sharing with them what they heard from Jesus.

John reminds us how Jesus engaged people in conversation with these words: "I have made known to you everything I heard from my Father" (John 15:15). I don't know the pastor or priest who is ready to tell all, but if we want a different outcome clergy have to tell more than they do now. Only then will lay people follow the example and do the same. When we engage in real conversation with others, they become friends that become a community that acts in concert to change things. Since I began organizing professionally, I have encouraged clergy to engage in conversation with one another and selected lay people whom they are called to serve. Jesus preached to the masses, and after the big delivery, he had intimate conversations with a select group of men and women that we refer to as his "disciples." Every time people witness clergy in conversation in a communal gathering, the "new disciples" are inspired to be community, to invite others into the conversation, and to focus on taking some constructive action together.

What is the different way to behave that will transform individuals and build community? Go to the well as Jesus did. Jesus wanted to know the Samaritan woman, saw the best in her when she presented her faults, and discovered their common ancestor and shared agenda in the teachings of Jacob. The Samaritan woman became an enthusiastic and powerful witness, a change agent in her neighborhood. Why? Jesus met her where she was, listened without condemning, and convinced her that he would accompany her on the journey. John reminds us that if we do as Jesus did, we can accomplish great things because we will become one with his Father (John 14:12). We not only become one with the Father, Son, and Holy Spirit, we become one with the others we engage in conversation. The Father's power lies in the community that is built when we engage in the art of accompaniment, the real conversations that take place on one another's turf. Power begins in the art of accompaniment, the conversations that unite people as Jesus' teachings brought people into conversation in the Upper Room.

Now what? I invite clergy to continue to meet and talk to each other, and invite lay people to join the conversation. Be encouraged. One day when I was lamenting about how difficult my life was because people were not ready to take any action, my wife asked me to look in the rear view mirror. I saw the $5,000,000 community recreation center that was the fruit of my initiating conversations years before. We drive two miles on the way to our next stop for the day, passing the high school with the renovated gym and the new football stadium and the $13,000,000 community library—all in the poorest ward in Washington, D.C. My wife asked me to reflect on what I saw. For each of these, I saw a pastor who engaged in a communal gathering with other clergy before engaging their congregations in conversation about what could be and should be if we lived the gospel. From these conversations, specific lay leaders emerged who brought the gospel to life in the neighborhood. It was the action of laity, working in concert with clergy and others, who got things done you could touch and see. Those clergy and the lay leaders they invited into the conversation should ride and reflect as I did with my wife's encouragement. When they ride and reflect, they look and say, "I can do more."

I am asking clergy to believe and do. Do what?

"Very truly, I tell you, the one who believes in me will also do the works that I do and, in fact, will do greater works than these, because I am going to the Father. I will do whatever you ask in my name, so that the Father may be glorified in the Son. If in my name you ask me for anything, I will do it" (John 14:12-14).

Jesus wants us, the descendants of the original disciples, to ask, pray, and do. If you are willing to try, then answer the two final questions on the next page.

The Scripture

Read John 14:12.

◼ ◼ ◼ ◼ ◼

The Questions

1. Who are the leaders in your midst that are poised to act on their faith in the neighborhood? List their names.

2. How and when will they and you begin the process of initiating conversations with those in your parish and community that will lead to communal action that transforms?

◼ ◼ ◼ ◼ ◼

This is not the end. If you answer the two questions, it is the beginning of building the new community. Walking with these newly discovered leaders, we can write the next chapter of the Acts of the Apostles.

This is an invitation to the readers to do something different. In organizing terminology, this is "an action." I want to improve your health. My message is this: "The joy is in the action." It sounds simple. We often imagine ourselves doing this but get busy and do many things that distract us from the right things. This is an invitation to practice ten concrete actions to leave the right message in the neighborhood:

1. ***Be deliberate and intentional about meeting leaders.*** Do as Jesus did; go to the well. I spoke to a leader who had a vision for marriage preparation and enrichment that was almost identical to the pastor's. After nine years of working in this ministry with this pastor, he did not think the pastor was interested in his work. The leader did not know his pastor; the pastor did not know him either. This is the norm in most parishes, a norm that must be changed.

2. ***Pick your team before you pick your battle.*** Moses picked Joshua to prevail against Amalek, and other men with specific talents to continue his mission. Joshua selected twelve to lead the tribes of Israel, continuing the work. Jesus had twelve leaders and other disciples that he got to know before he engaged in public action. Too often, we forget the way that Moses and Jesus did it and attempt to go it alone.

3. *Invite people to participate in the six focused conversations.* This is the essence of the communal life. Listen to hear stories of encounters with the living Christ, to discover leaders and the important battles to be fought to build the community.

4. *Take action on what you hear in the focused conversations.* If we practice living the communal life, every action will be consistent with the teachings of the apostles. We really meet leaders when we take the communal action. Watch them come out of the woodwork and grow.

5. *Plan before and reflect after every action.* Jesus made a habit of inviting the twelve to sit with him to review the parable after the teaching moment to make sure they understood and could apply the lesson at the critical moment. We must do the same.

6. *Rest and reflect on the Sabbath.* God (the Father, Son, and Holy Spirit) took a day to look out over his creation and reflect on what he had done. When we rest and reflect once a week as God did, Jesus comes to life where we are and our lives are transformed. Jesus is the Church, which is love in action to transform the world.

7. *Live in a "Catholic" culture.* Culture is that which dominates a parish. Many who read this can remember the story of a day when every adult felt a "holy obligation" to discipline every child in the community,

people rallied to build a collective to meet the emergent need of the day, and good things happened even when people didn't have money. This is the culture and practice described in Acts 2:42.

8. *Act in concert with those with whom we share the faith.* Christians baptize "in the name of the Father, Son, and Holy Spirit." Jesus was formed in the Jewish tradition. Muslims share the belief in the one God. We encounter others who, regardless of religious practice, are sincere in the search for the truth. The concerted action was a core belief of the community that formed Dr. King, the first African-American bishops, and the ordinary folk who were the heroes of the Civil Rights movement. They were not all Black or all Catholic, but were honest in their quest for the truth.

9. *Make a habit of beginning with a reflection on the living word of God.* I like Scripture, especially the selected texts in the Liturgy of the Hours. It may also be good to have someone from the assembly share a personal encounter with the risen Christ for reflection. This proves that Christ is alive in the world.

10. *Stay focused on the big question:* "How is my individual action with this assembly helping to build the communal life in the parish and the neighborhood?"

I have had the privilege of sitting regularly with a group of pastors who are striving to recommit to living the communal life as one Church. When the twelfth pastor came to join the communal assembly, things took off. Clergy and lay people in our area are excited about their Catholic faith and are satisfying the hunger for the communal life and witnessing to their encounter with the risen Christ. It looks like the assembled are ready to break out of the Upper Room to write the next Chapter of Acts. The next step for you, the reader, is to join in the conversation, begin to practice the art of accompaniment, break out of the Upper Room, and go out into your parish and neighborhood to take action.

■ ■ ■ ■ ■

Read and watch our Holy Father Francis. Two of my favorite people, C. S. Lewis and Malcolm X, were avid readers and great teachers. I have my own habits of highly effective people, and reading is first among them, taught by family and reinforced by my favorite folk. We do physical things to exercise and improve our bodies; we read to stimulate our minds and imaginations. If you want to know something of yourself and be the person God calls you to be, develop a reading list for yourself and continue to build upon it. Here is my list for today.

Alan Jacobs. *The Narnian: The Life and Imagination of C. S. Lewis.* New York: Harper Collins Publishers, 2005.

C. S. Lewis was a great communicator. With more than 600,000 published pages, he is among the most prolific writers ever. The great communicator still appeals to children and adults as well. He excelled in writing compelling, cogent, and easy-to-understand stories about living a principled life.

James Baldwin. *The Fire Next Time*. New York: The Dial Press, 1962, 1963.

Malcolm X said that Baldwin was not invited to speak at the March on Washington because people were not ready to hear the truth. If you want your children to understand the truth in love, read Baldwin's "Letter to My Nephew," the first essay in the book. When most anticipated anger, Baldwin spoke with love.

* * * * *

Rev Austin Flannery, O.P., General Editor. *The Basic Sixteen Documents Vatican Council II*. Northport: Costello Publishing Company, 1996.

The best articulation of the "world as it should be" was produced by the Catholic Church and recorded in the documents of Vatican II. This is the Church at its best and you do not have to be Catholic to appreciate the words, written fifty years ago, that are equally applicable to living faith in the world today.

* * * * *

Manning Marable. *Malcolm X: A Life of Reinvention*. New York: The Penguin Group, 2011.

Malcolm X is arguably the best example of the Church's teaching on progressive conversion. His transformation from street hustler to citizen of the world is worth studying. It was interesting to read that J. Edgar Hoover's FBI found the religious Malcolm as a man with no exploitable vices. Few, if any people, received that type of evaluation from the FBI.

Rev Gregory Boyle, SJ. *Tattoos On The Heart.* New York: Free Press, 2010.

The Jesuits are the largest religious order in the Catholic Church and are known for living on the edge. Father Boyle shows what could be when you take the Church into the neighborhood. If you want to see how love can transform in the most difficult circumstances, read this treatise on finding Christ in the roughest neighborhoods.

Rev Uwem Akpan, SJ. *Say You're One of Them.* New York: Little, Brown &Company, 2008.

This is fiction based on real-life struggles in Africa. You cannot appreciate joy unless you have a real experience of human suffering. Want to be introduced to the people of our day with whom Jesus identified? Meet them here; discover courage and hope in suffering; and make a commitment to transform the world.

Tupak Shakur. *The Rose That Grew From Concrete.* New York: Pocket Books, 1999.

My son told me to read something different—poetry from someone who is different from you. Often the best teacher is the one who is most different from you. Tupak was a deep thinker and force for love in the neighborhood. He is a reminder that the one with his hat on backwards can be among the most forward thinkers in the neighborhood.

▓ ▓ ▓ ▓ ▓

Malcolm Gladwell. *The Tipping Point.* New York: Little, Brown & Company, 2000, 2002. *The Outliers.* London: Penguin Group, 2008.

Gladwell's writings are treated as a two-volume book. Together they give a picture of building a collective that is focused on accomplishing a mission. Gladwell says it takes three to five years of consistent study and practice to develop as a professional and that the development process is never complete.

▓ ▓ ▓ ▓ ▓

Rabbi Harold Kushner. *Who Needs God?* New York: Summit Books, 1989.

The rabbi makes a convincing rational argument for the existence of God in the world. The recent leaders of the Catholic Church talk about relativism as the enemy; a Jewish leader makes the case for morals and the need for believing in an immutable truth that is universally applicable. This book is another reminder of the value in looking for the good in the one who is different from you.

M. Scott Peck. *The Road Less Traveled.* New York: Touchstone, 1978.

I read the original and the twenty-fifth anniversary edition and discovered that much of what I retained about love, religion, discipline, and delayed gratification or self-denial was included in this book. Peck makes the case for real love, which is being the best you can be so that you can discover and bring out the best in others.

USING THE TOOLS OF EFFECTIVE ORGANIZING TO BUILD YOUR UNION LOCAL'S STRENGTH
by Jonathan Lange and Michael Gecan
This booklet, by two of the top organizers in the Metro Industrial Areas Foundation, lays out how four of the basic organizing tools used in successful community organizing can be adapted and used by labor unions both to rebuild their membership and leadership and to establish needed relationships with outside institutions and organizations that can help them achieve their mutual self-interests. 52 pages, paperback

GOING PUBLIC
An Organizer's Guide to Citizen Action
by Michael Gecan
Mike Gecan, the co-executive director of the Industrial Areas Foundation and Metro IAF, tells stories and teaches lessons from his lifetime in community organizing. He explores the difference between "public" and "private," and the critical importance of building relationships as the basis for all successful, long-term organizing.
192 pages, paperback

WHAT IS SOCIAL JUSTICE?
by William L. Droel
A primer by Bill Droel of the National Center for the Laity on the difference between social justice and charity, commutative justice, and distributive justice. Explains that social justice is a virtue that is practiced mostly by "insiders" of institutions, sometimes with a little help from "outsiders," and must result in the act of organizing if it is to come to fruition. 42 pages, paperback

REFLECTING WITH SCRIPTURE
ON COMMUNITY ORGANIZING
by Rev. Jeff Krehbiel
The pastor of the Church of the Pilgrims in Washington, D.C., and co-chair of the Washington Interfaith Network offers reflections on four passages from Scripture and how they relate to the experience of community organizing. He also offers a Group Study Guide for congregational use. 60 pages, paperback

EFFECTIVE ORGANIZING
FOR CONGREGATIONAL RENEWAL
by Michael Gecan
The author of *Going Public* and co-executive director of the Industrial Areas Foundation describes how the tools of organizing can and are transforming Protestant, Catholic, Jewish and Muslim congregations. Included are five case studies of congregations that have used this process to grow. 54 pages, paperback

REBUILDING OUR INSTITUTIONS
by Ernesto Cortes, Jr.
Ernie Cortes, the co-executive director of the Industrial Areas Foundation, argues that community organizing cultivates the practices needed for democracy to thrive, including one-on-one relational meetings, house meetings, and systematic reflection on them afterwards. This book contains several examples from organizations in California, Louisiana, and Texas that helped local congregations and other mediating institutions identify, confront, and change things that were destroying their families and communities. 30 pages, paperback